English for the Thoughtful Child

GReenleaf
P · R · E · S · S

First Printing, February 2003
Revised for POD, May 2013

Greenleaf Press
www.greenleafpress.com
1570 Old Laguardo Road, Lebanon, TN 37087

English for the Thoughtful Child

Fred Scott & Gordon Southworth
revised and edited by Cynthia A. Shearer

Greenleaf Press

Lebanon, Tennessee

Contents

Introduction vii

To the Teacher ix

Lesson 1 1
Picture Lesson: Morning Call

Lesson 2 2
Kinds of Sentences

Lesson 3 4
Practice in Writing Statements

Lesson 4 7
Practice in Writing Paragraphs

Lesson 5 9
Practice in Writing Questions

Lesson 6 11
Nature Lesson: Cats

Lesson 7 13
Homonyms

Lesson 8 15
More Homonyms

Lesson 9 17
A Story to Tell

Lesson 10 18
Copy Work

Table of Contents (continued)

Lesson 11 20
Practice in Writing Exclamations

Lesson 12 22
Nature Lesson: Butterflies

Lesson 13 23
Picture Lesson: The Butterfly Hunters

Lesson 14 24
A Fable to Narrate

Lesson 15 25
Contractions

Lesson 16 28
Common and Proper Nouns

Lesson 17 31
Possessive Nouns

Lesson 18 35
Plural or Possessive Nouns

Lesson 19 37
A Poem to Learn

Lesson 20 38
Picture Lesson: Frank's Birthday Present

Lesson 21 39
Practice in Writing Quotations

Lesson 22 42
Practice in Writing Divided Quotations

Lesson 23 45
Practice in Writing Conversations

Table of Contents (continued)

Lesson 24 47
Nature Lesson: The Baltimore Oriole

Lesson 25 49
Nouns Made Plural by Adding -es

Lesson 26 51
More Plural or Possessive Nouns

Lesson 27 54
A Poem to Study

Lesson 28 55
Synonyms

Lesson 29 57
Choosing the Best Word

Lesson 30 59
Review

Lesson 31 63
Picture Lesson: Amusing a Child

Lesson 32 64
Plural Possessive Nouns

Lesson 33 66
Stories to Narrate

Lesson 34 67
Nature Lesson: Barn Swallows

Lesson 35 68
A Poem to Copy

Lesson 36 69
Practice in Using *Who's* and *Whose*

Table of Contents (continued)

Lesson 37 70
Practice in Using Commas in a Series

Lesson 38 72
Plural Possesive Nouns Review

Lesson 39 73
Plural Nouns Ending in -ies

Lesson 40 76
Picture Lesson: The Soldier and the Bear

Lesson 41 77
There, Their, and They're

Lesson 42 80
More Practice in Writing Conversations

Lesson 43 82
Fourteen Plural Nouns Ending in -ves

Lesson 44 87
Nature Lesson: The Rabbit's Home

Lesson 45 88
A Poem to Read Aloud

Lesson 46 90
Writing the Titles of Long Works

Lesson 47 92
Writing the Titles of Short Works

Lesson 48 94
Copy Work

Lesson 49 95
Dictation Review

Table of Contents (continued)

Lesson 50 96
Picture Lesson: Helping Mother

Lesson 51 97
Practice in Writing Friendly Letters

Lesson 52 99
Practice in Addressing Envelopes

Lesson 53 100
A Letter to Write

Lesson 54 101
Irregular Plural Nouns

Lesson 55 104
Making Irregular Plural Nouns Possessive

Lesson 56 106
Nature Lesson: The Harvest Mouse

Lesson 57 108
A Poem to Learn

Lesson 58 109
Review of Plural Nouns

Lesson 59 111
Dictation Review

Lesson 60 112
Picture Lesson: A Heavy Load

Appendix 113
Internet Resources for Selected Nature Lessons

Introduction

Adapted from the original "Note to Teachers" from Lessons in English: Book One, *by Fred Newton Scott and Gordon A. Southworth, 1913.*

[This book presupposes] a wise and capable teacher who will use [it] with the attainments and needs of her pupils in mind, omitting here and supplementing there according to varying conditions.

Too many teachers think of a textbook as a kind of machine gun, built to fire so many loads a minute with deadly precision. This is a vicious error. A textbook should be the teacher's friend, guide, and helper. It may be a powerful aid and resource, but it can never take the place of the teacher's personal enthusiasm, sympathy, and stimulus.

In [this book] teachers will find a great variety of material which they can use in accordance with their best judgment. Exercises are given for copying, for dictation, for rewriting, for description, for letter writing, for recording the results of observation and experience, for the use of words and their synonyms, and for practice in the use of correct forms. Selections from the best literature are given to be studied and learned, and to furnish suggestions for kindred work from the school readers. Ample provision is made for the correlation of nature work with language, and the elements of grammar are inductively presented.

The inductive method has been followed throughout. A right use of the suggestive questions will lead to habits of thought, observation, and investigation along given lines. Other questions may be added, but the direct imparting of information will not often be necessary.

Oral lessons should precede and outnumber written lessons. Each exercise should be the subject of conversation and study before any attempt is made to write it.

A special effort should be made by the teacher to see that the child's thought is clear and distinct in his own mind. The first thoughts of children are, and perhaps ought to be, more or less hazy. It is the business of the teacher of English to dissipate the fog, to disentangle the confused ideas, to induce habits of clear and orderly thinking. Much can be accomplished toward this end by training the child from the start to grasp firmly the units of discourse, the sentence, the paragraph, and the whole of composition. This does not mean that the children are to learn to talk about these things, but that they must somehow gradually acquire the sense of them.

A final word of caution may not be out of place. Teachers of English are apt to attach much importance to the formal side of their instruction, and to assume that pupils' facility in reciting rules and detecting errors of speech is a sure sign of progress. The end of all instruction in English is growth in power of expression and appreciation. Drill which contributes to this end is good. Drill which, falling short of this end, merely fills the child's mind with rules and symbols, is a grievous waste of time.

To the Teacher

English for the Thoughtful Child 2 has been a long time in coming. Since the publication of the first book (*English for the Thoughtful Child*), many have asked whether there would be other books in the series. Over the years I have made several attempts at a second book, but never felt like I was headed in the right direction. If it wasn't going to be a book I could be excited about using with my own children, I wasn't interested in inflicting it on other families and other children.

I am happy to say that I am excited about this second volume. It is based largely on the book *Lessons in English: Book One*, by Fred Newton Scott and Gordon A. Southworth (originally published by Ben J. H. Sanborn and Company in 1913), though it has been drastically rearranged and supplemented.

Like the original *English for the Thoughtful Child*, the focus of this book is on the development of a child's composition skills. The grammatical content is subordinate to that goal. In addition to composition exercises, there are narration exercises, poems, and selections which may be used as either copy or memory work.

Those who like to keep notebooks may wish to divide their notebooks into sections for copy work, written narratives, dictation, and composition. With each picture lesson, I recommend spending a good amount of time studying and discussing the picture. Use the questions suggested for the picture as a starting point and a guide, not a script. As your student talks about all he sees in the picture, you have an opportunity to informally walk him through the planning stage of writing, the pre-writing stage, in which possible details are listed, sketched out, ordered, and explored before actual writing starts.

Before a student is asked to write an original story, he should be comfortable with the basic physical work of handwriting and be able to spell most of the words he will want to use. A child who is focused on the act of handwriting, or is constantly stopping to ask how simple words are spelled, will not be able focus on the real assignment: composition. These children need to be able to dictate their stories (and their narrations) to you. Once the story is written, read it aloud together and have the student copy it in his own handwriting.

Do all that you can to preserve the fun that should be part of writing. Some children will take to writing more enthusiastically than others. Children who are exposed to good literature will find that composition comes more easily to them.

Some children will have to be encouraged to stop writing, others will need coaxing and encouragement to start.

The writing most likely to come from the picture lessons will be narrative or descriptive. Through the nature lessons, students have an opportunity to develop expository skills. If your students keep nature notebooks, these lessons can be done in connection with those notebooks. References to Anna Comstock's *Handbook of Nature Study* have been provided where possible, but it is not intended to be your only resource. You might use these lessons to teach students to use library and reference materials, including encyclopedias and Internet sources. Web sites which have information on wildlife found in your area, such as www.enature.com, can be great resources. In the back of the book you will find an appendix listing sites related to some of the nature lessons.

Most importantly, train your students to develop observation skills as they study the natural world around them. After your students have read, listened, observed, and drawn pictures of the subject of the lesson at hand, give them a chance to tell what they have learned.

This book simply would not have happened without the encouragement and support of many people. I am thankful for the many afternoons when my oldest son, Jon, and his most wonderful wife, Sarah, entertained all my younger children so I could hide in the office and write. Credit must also go to Greenleaf's incredible graphic designer, Alyson Fitch, who ever-so-patiently put up with all the false starts and the seemingly endless rearrangements of lessons. And many thanks to those family and friends whose prayers kept me going; to my dear children, who continue to be their mom's beloved guinea pigs; and to their dad, my best friend and (most of the time) my sanity.

Cyndy Shearer, 2003

Lesson 1
PICTURE LESSON: MORNING CALL

Study the picture. Talk with your teacher about the scene.

The dog is about to wake the little girl. When she awakens she will say something to him. What will she say if she is glad to see him? What will she say if she is vexed? What question might she ask him? What command might she give? If you were to ask her what the dog's name is, what would she say? What would she say if the dog barked sharply at her? If the dog could speak, what might he say in reply? If her mother came into the room, would her mother pet or scold the dog? How old do you think the girl is? What would the mother and daughter talk about?

EXERCISE
On a separate sheet of paper, write a story about the little girl and her dog. Why is the dog so eager for the little girl to get up? What is about to happen?

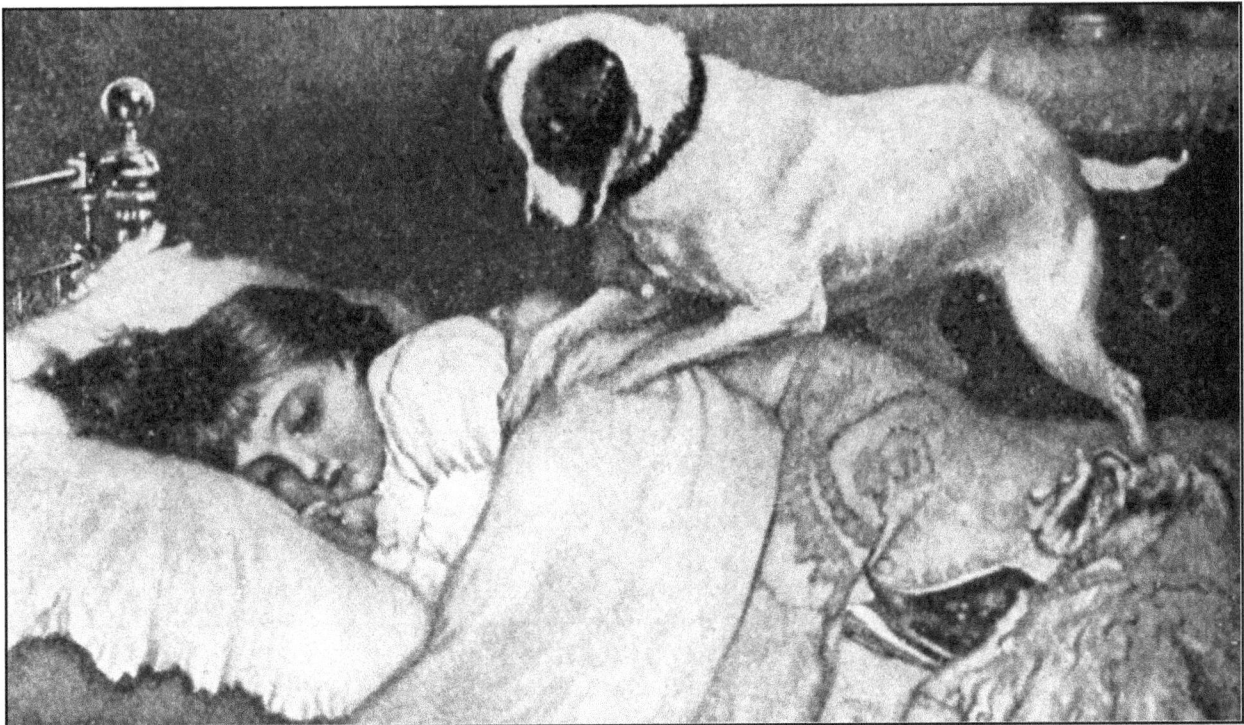

Lesson 2
KINDS OF SENTENCES

[Several questions in Lesson 2 reference the picture in Lesson 1.]

When we talk or write, the words that belong together and fall naturally into groups are called **sentences**. There are different kinds of sentences.

Some sentences **tell**, or **state** something.
What might the mother tell her little girl? What might the little girl tell her mother?

Some sentences **ask questions**.
What questions might the little girl's mother ask when she enters the room?
What questions might the girl ask?

In some sentences, someone is **commanded** or **requested** to do something.
What command might the little girl give to the dog?
What request might she make of her mother?

EXERCISE
Tell which of the following sentences make a statement, ask a question, or contain a command. Write either **statement**, **question**, *or* **command** *on the line after each sentence.*

1. What is the name of this picture? _____

2. The name of the artist is C. B. Barber. _____

3. Look carefully at the face of the dog. _____

4. What time of day is it? _____

5. The child is not afraid of the dog. _____

6. It is time to get up. _____

7. Have you slept well? ——————————————————

8. Where does the dog sleep? ——————————————

A period should be placed at the end of a **command** or **statement**.

A question mark should be placed at the end of a **question**.

Lesson 3
PRACTICE IN WRITING STATEMENTS

EXERCISE 1

Little children are always asking questions. Suppose that your little brother or sister asked these questions. How would you answer?

1. What can horses do?
2. Of what use are cows?
3. What is the use of a watch?
4. What does a farmer do with a plow?
5. What does the postman do with the letters we give him?

Now write the statements you have made.

1. _____

_____

2. _____

_____

3. _____

_____

4. _____

_____

5. _____

_____

EXERCISE 2

Suppose your little brother or sister asked you about what things are. First give your answer orally, then write it.

1. What is a thimble? _____

_____

2. What is a minnow? _____

_____

3. What are marbles? _____

_____

4. What is veal? _____

_____

5. What is a needle? _____

_____

EXERCISE 3

Suppose that the questions were about the making of things. First give your answer orally, then write it.

1. Of what are shoes made? _____

_____

2. Who made your coat? _____

_____

3. Who built your house? _____

_____

4. Of what is candy made? _____

_____

5. Who makes doors? _____

_____

6. Of what is bread made? _____

_____

7. Of what is butter made? _____

_____

Lesson 4
PRACTICE IN WRITING PARAGRAPHS

When we write as we should, the sentences that belong together fall naturally into groups called **paragraphs**. All the sentences in a paragraph should talk about the same subject. When we begin to talk about a new subject, we should begin a new paragraph.

To show that a new paragraph has been started, the first line starts five letter spaces further to the right than the other lines. Always leave a space the width of two letters between the sentences in a paragraph when writing.

Boys and girls are very likely to join their sentences together by using **and** at the beginning of each statement. If you find that you are starting sentences in your paragraph with **and**, take the **and** out and let the next word start a new sentence. Make sure all the sentences in your paragraph speak about the same subject and are complete thoughts.

EXERCISE 1
Read this story.

How to Get Breakfast

It was early one summer morning. There were four little chickens in a group. They were all peeping. One would have liked a fresh green leaf. Another was hungry for some sweet yellow meal. The third was waiting for some kind of bug. A nice fat worm would have made the fourth one happy.

The four little chickens looked at one another fretfully, and began to chirp. It sounded as if they said, "We're hungry! We want our breakfast! Why doesn't somebody come and give us our breakfast?"

Then the mother hen, in the garden close by, clucked and fluttered, as if to say, "If you want any breakfast you must come here and scratch!"

How many paragraphs did you find? Where does the first word of each paragraph begin? What does the first paragraph speak about? What is the second paragraph about? What is the last paragraph about?

EXERCISE 2

On another sheet of paper, write this story from memory in your own words.

Lesson 5
PRACTICE IN WRITING QUESTIONS

What is a **question**? How must it begin and end? How many questions were asked in the last lesson? How can you tell they were questions?

Draw a question mark here. _____

A question should begin with a **capital letter** and end with a **question mark** (**?**).

EXERCISE 1

1. *Make a statement about a clock.* _____

_____

2. *Ask a question about a clock.* _____

_____

3. *Make a statement about rain.* _____

_____

4. *Ask a question about rain.* _____

_____

5. *Answer your question about a clock.* _____

_____

6. *Answer your question about rain.* ⎯⎯⎯⎯⎯⎯⎯⎯⎯⎯⎯⎯⎯⎯⎯⎯⎯⎯

⎯⎯⎯⎯⎯⎯⎯⎯⎯⎯⎯⎯⎯⎯⎯⎯⎯⎯⎯⎯⎯⎯⎯⎯⎯⎯⎯⎯⎯⎯⎯⎯⎯⎯⎯⎯⎯⎯

EXERCISE 2

Think of something you would like to know about each of the following things, then ask your questions orally.

water	frogs	raisins	wind	this book
vacation	sugar	milk	robins	

EXERCISE 3

Choose one of the questions you asked in Exercise 2. Find the answer to your question, then write it on the lines below.

⎯⎯⎯⎯⎯⎯⎯⎯⎯⎯⎯⎯⎯⎯⎯⎯⎯⎯⎯⎯⎯⎯⎯⎯⎯⎯⎯⎯⎯⎯⎯⎯⎯⎯⎯⎯⎯⎯

⎯⎯⎯⎯⎯⎯⎯⎯⎯⎯⎯⎯⎯⎯⎯⎯⎯⎯⎯⎯⎯⎯⎯⎯⎯⎯⎯⎯⎯⎯⎯⎯⎯⎯⎯⎯⎯⎯

⎯⎯⎯⎯⎯⎯⎯⎯⎯⎯⎯⎯⎯⎯⎯⎯⎯⎯⎯⎯⎯⎯⎯⎯⎯⎯⎯⎯⎯⎯⎯⎯⎯⎯⎯⎯⎯⎯

⎯⎯⎯⎯⎯⎯⎯⎯⎯⎯⎯⎯⎯⎯⎯⎯⎯⎯⎯⎯⎯⎯⎯⎯⎯⎯⎯⎯⎯⎯⎯⎯⎯⎯⎯⎯⎯⎯

⎯⎯⎯⎯⎯⎯⎯⎯⎯⎯⎯⎯⎯⎯⎯⎯⎯⎯⎯⎯⎯⎯⎯⎯⎯⎯⎯⎯⎯⎯⎯⎯⎯⎯⎯⎯⎯⎯

⎯⎯⎯⎯⎯⎯⎯⎯⎯⎯⎯⎯⎯⎯⎯⎯⎯⎯⎯⎯⎯⎯⎯⎯⎯⎯⎯⎯⎯⎯⎯⎯⎯⎯⎯⎯⎯⎯

⎯⎯⎯⎯⎯⎯⎯⎯⎯⎯⎯⎯⎯⎯⎯⎯⎯⎯⎯⎯⎯⎯⎯⎯⎯⎯⎯⎯⎯⎯⎯⎯⎯⎯⎯⎯⎯⎯

Lesson 6
NATURE LESSON: CATS

Study the picture. Talk about it with your teacher. You might answer these questions:

1. Why can the cat climb the tree so easily?
2. Why cannot the dogs climb too?
3. How many claws has the cat?
4. If your fingers and toes were all claws, would you have more claws than the cat has?
5. Has she the same number of claws on her forepaws as on her hind paws?
6. How many claws has a dog?
7. How are they different from a cat's claws?
8. Where are a cat's claws when she is not using them?
9. Why does a cat make no noise when walking?
10. What kind of noise are these dogs making?
11. What kind of noise is this cat making?
12. What might each dog say if he could speak?
13. What might the cat say?
14. If the cat sees a little boy coming to help her down, will she make a different noise?
15. How will it sound?
16. Of what use is the cat to the boy?
17. Of what use are the dogs?
18. Do you know what is meant by a *domestic animal*?
19. Notice the dog on the left. Is he the dog that awakened the little girl in the picture on page 1?

EXERCISE
Choose five of the questions you discussed with your teacher and write the answers to them on the following lines.

11

1. _____

_____

2. _____

_____

3. _____

_____

4. _____

_____

5. _____

_____

Lesson 7
HOMONYMS

Words that sound alike but differ in meaning are called **homonyms**.

Circle the homonyms in this sentence.

Before you write, choose the right word.

EXERCISE 1
Choose from the following words to complete each of the four sentences below.

rode	are	blue	flower	ate
blew	flour	road	eight	our

1. _____ pints make a gallon.

2. **The golden-rod is an autumn** _____ .

3. **What makes the sky** _____?

4. **Which of you** _____ to town?

EXERCISE 2
Write words pronounced like each of these, but differently spelled. Tell your teacher what each word means.

sew _____   raze _____

mane _____   weighs _____

vain _____

13

EXERCISE 3

Write four statements and four questions, using one of the following words in each sentence.

cent	grate	our	bear	pale
sent	great	hour	bare	pail

1. _____

_____

2. _____

_____

3. _____

_____

4. _____

_____

5. _____

_____

6. _____

_____

7. _____

_____

8. _____

Lesson 8
MORE HOMONYMS

EXERCISE 1

Write five statements and five questions, using one of the following words in each sentence.

led	no	meat	new	wood
lead	know	meet	knew	would

1. _____

_____

2. _____

_____

3. _____

_____

4. _____

_____

5. _____

_____

6. _____

_____

7. _____

8. _____

_____

9. _____

_____

10. _____

_____

EXERCISE 2

Think of a homonym for each of the following words.

bin _____   pane _____   right _____   see _____

son _____   pair _____   sew _____   red _____

lain _____   sale _____   sum _____   bough _____

EXERCISE 3

On another sheet of paper, make a list of other words that sound alike, but differ in meaning.

EXERCISE 4

On another sheet of paper, write sentences for five of the homonyms you listed in Exercise 2.

Lesson 9
A STORY TO TELL

This cat has been sent to a little girl as a birthday present from her uncle. The cat has come safely on an airplane, rested after her long journey, and now is looking about for someone to play with. You may imagine that the little girl is just coming into the room to see the present her father and mother so carefully hid from her the night before. What will she say when she sees the cat, and what will she do?

EXERCISE

First tell and then write the story of "Kitten's Trip to Her New Home," as the kitten might tell it if she could speak. Write your story on a separate sheet of paper.

Lesson 10
COPY WORK

This painting, *Head of a Child*, is by the great artist Leonardo da Vinci.

What is the little one thinking about?
Very wonderful things, no doubt!
    Unwritten history!
    Unfathomed mystery!
Yet he laughs and cries, and eats and drinks,
And chuckles and crows, and nods and winks,
As if his head were as full of kinks
And curious riddles as any sphinx!

Now he thinks he'll go to sleep!
I can see the shadow creep
Over his eyes, in soft eclipse,
Over his brow, and o'er his lips,
Out to his little finger-tips!
Softly sinking, down he goes!
Down he goes! down he goes!
See! he is hushed in sweet repose!

J. G. Holland

OUR BABY

No shoes to hide her tiny toes,
    No stockings on her feet;
Her supple ankles white as snow,
    Or early blossoms sweet.

Her simple dress of sprinkled pink,
    Her double, dimpled chin;
Her puckered lip and bonny mouth,
    With not a tooth between.

Her eyes so like her mother's eyes,
    Two gentle, liquid things;
Her face is like an angel's face,
    We're glad she has no wings!

Author Unknown

EXERCISE

Copy one of the these selections onto another sheet of paper. If your teacher asks you to, learn it and recite it.

Lesson 11
PRACTICE IN WRITING EXCLAMATIONS

Read the following sentences to your teacher.

There is a cow.
There is a cow!

Imagine you are riding down a country road, passing farm after farm, and your mother asks, "What do you see out the window?" Would you answer with the first or the second sentence?

If you walked out of your bedroom into your living room and saw a large cow standing in front of the sofa, which sentence would you be most likely to say to your mother?

A sentence that shows strong emotion or surprise is called an **exclamation.** Exclamations end with an **exclamation mark** (**!**).

EXERCISE
Write what you might exclaim if these things happened to you.

1. If you heard a crash of thunder _____

_____

2. If you saw a kitten turn over an ink bottle _____

_____

3. If, turning a corner, you met your best friend unexpectedly _____

_____

4. If you narrowly escaped being run over _____

_____

5. If your foot went to sleep _____

_____

6. If you received a present of a million dollars _____

_____

7. If you heard a fire alarm _____

_____

Lesson 12
NATURE LESSON: BUTTERFLIES

[While it is possible, and best, to combine this lesson with a study of butterflies in their natural homes, it may also be done indoors out of season. For background information, see *Handbook of Nature Study* by Anna Comstock, pages 301-310. Many excellent books on butterflies are available at libraries as well. Suggested Internet supplements for this lesson can be found in the Internet Resources appendix.]

Swallowtail and Monarch butterflies are large and brightly colored. Like all insects, their bodies are divided into three parts: the head, the thorax, and the abdomen. Butterflies' beautiful wings and graceful flight make them many people's favorite insect. Your teacher will read you more information about one of these varieties of butterfly, or will show you where you can find more information.

EXERCISE 1
Draw a picture of a swallowtail or a monarch butterfly, then write a short paragraph describing its appearance.

EXERCISE 2
Write a short conversation that might take place between a swallowtail caterpillar and a bird, showing why the bird will not eat this caterpillar.

Lesson 13
PICTURE LESSON: THE BUTTERFLY HUNTERS

These three children are hunting butterflies. What names would you give each of the three? Where did they catch the butterflies? How long do you think they have been out? How did they capture the big handsome butterfly? What kind of butterfly is it? Did anything funny happen during their hunt? Tell about it.

EXERCISE

On another sheet of paper, write a story about these "butterfly hunters."

Lesson 14
A FABLE TO NARRATE

A **fable** is a story or tale that teaches a lesson or moral.

Read this fable.

THE HUMMINGBIRD AND THE BUTTERFLY

A hummingbird met a butterfly. Being pleased with the butterfly's beauty and the glory of his wings, she proposed that they should always be friends.

"I cannot think of it," said the butterfly, "for you once spurned me and called me a crawling dolt."

"Impossible!" exclaimed the hummingbird. "I have always had the highest respect for such beautiful creatures as you."

"You may now," said the butterfly, "but when you insulted me, I was a caterpillar. So let me give you a piece of advice: Never insult the humble. It is rude and unkind; besides, they may be better than they seem."

EXERCISE 1
On a separate sheet of paper, write the story of the hummingbird and the butterfly from memory.

EXERCISE 2
Tell your teacher the lesson taught by this fable.

Lesson 15
CONTRACTIONS

Read the following sentences.

Frank is not here.   Frank isn't here.
I was not absent.   I wasn't absent.
Mary has not gone.   Mary hasn't gone.

Answer these questions with your teacher.

1. Which pairs of sentences mean the same things?
2. How is each pair different?
3. How do we make **isn't** from **is not**?
4. Of what two words is **wasn't** made?
5. What letter is omitted in the short (or **contracted**) form of **is not**, **was not**, and **has not**?
6. What takes the place of this letter?

In a **contraction**, an **apostrophe** (') takes the place of the letter or letters left out.

Example: **Has not** becomes **hasn't**, and **cannot** becomes **can't**.

Tell your teacher which of the following things you would be more likely to say if you were talking with a friend.

I am not coming!   I'm not coming!
That is not mine.   That's not mine.

In casual conversation, we normally use contractions. When we speak or write in more formal settings, contractions are not normally used.

EXERCISE 1

Write the contractions of the following expressions.

is not _____   had not _____

was not _____   have not _____

would not _____   do not _____

does not _____   has not _____

EXERCISE 2

Use the contraction of each word pair in a statement.

1. is not _____

_____

2. was not _____

_____

3. would not _____

_____

4. does not _____

_____

5. did not _____

_____

EXERCISE 3

Use the contraction of each word pair in a question.

1. had not _____

_____

2. have not _____

_____

3. do not _____

_____

4. has not _____

_____

Lesson 16
COMMON AND PROPER NOUNS

A word that tells the name of a **person**, **place**, or **thing** is called a **noun**.

Underline the words that name **people**. *Circle* the words that name **places**. *Draw a box* around the words that name **things**.

dog	boy	girl	box
house	river	city	state
country	man	aunt	car

Read the following sentences with your teacher.

A young boy lives next door to me.
I studied about a small country.
My new puppy is a golden retriever.

Do the sentences you just read tell the names of a specific boy, country, and puppy?

Complete each sentence with the name of a specific boy, country and puppy.

_____ lives next door to me.

I studied about _____ .

_____ is a golden retriever.

Nouns that tell the name of a **specific** person, place, or thing are called **proper nouns**.

Proper nouns should begin with a **capital letter**.

Nouns that **do not** tell the name of a **specific** person, place or thing are called **common nouns**.

Common nouns **do not** begin with capital letters.

EXERCISE 1

*Read the list of words below. Tell whether each word is a common or a proper noun. Write a **P** in front of the **proper nouns**, and a **C** in front of the **common nouns**.*

Example: __C__ cow

_____ Matthew   _____ town   _____ George Washington

_____ teacher   _____ cat   _____ river

EXERCISE 2

Read the list of words below. If the word is a common noun, give a proper noun to go with it. If the word is a proper noun, give a common noun to go with it.

Example: **cow** __Bessy__

Madeline _____   girl _____

Matthew _____   town _____

George Washington _____   teacher _____

cat _____   river _____

EXERCISE 3

Write the following correctly from dictation.

1. John Thomas loves fresh tomatoes in the summer.
2. Canada, Mexico, and the United States are countries in North America.
3. The Red River runs through Texas.
4. Paul likes to swim in the river.

Lesson 17
POSSESSIVE NOUNS

Read these sentences with your teacher.

    John has a cart.
    John's cart is old.
    The cart's wheels move slowly.

1. What is said in the first statement?
2. What is said about the cart in the second statement?
3. What is said about the wheels in the third statement?
4. Who owns the cart? How do you know?
5. To what do the wheels belong? How do you know?

When a word is used to show to whom or to what something belongs, that word is said to denote (show) **possession** (ownership).

    The girl's hat was yellow.
    The doctor's horse ran across the bridge.
    There is the garden spider's web.

1. Whose hat is yellow? _____

2. Whose horse ran? _____

3. Whose web is that? _____

When we add an apostrophe (') and the letter -s to a singular noun or to a name, we are forming a singular possessive noun.

31

EXERCISE 1

Write sentences containing the following phrases.

      1. Helen's letter   4. the lady's glove
      2. a girl's shoe   5. the squirrel's teeth
      3. a day's work   6. the man's teeth

1. _____

_____

2. _____

_____

3. _____

_____

4. _____

_____

5. _____

_____

6. _____

_____

EXERCISE 2

Use the singular possessive forms of these nouns in sentences.

boy   Milly   pony   city

1. _____

_____

2. _____

_____

3. _____

_____

4. _____

_____

EXERCISE 3

Copy these sentences, filling in the blanks with names to show to whom or to what the object belongs.

1. This is Dr. _____ horse and carriage.

2. Where is Mr. _____ house?

3. _____ sister is much older than mine.

4. _____ drawing is prettier than _____ .

5. The song is sweeter than the _____ .

33

6. The _____ tongue is rough.

7. The _____ blood is cold.

EXERCISE 4
Listen as you teacher reads each of these sentences one time, then write them correctly on a separate piece of paper.

1. Franklin's kite was made of silk.
2. Hasn't Mr. Stone heard the news?
3. Our friend's letter must be answered.
4. Are not two mistakes too many?
5. Charles's pen doesn't write.

Lesson 18
PLURAL OR POSSESSIVE NOUNS

That farmer's trees are loaded with apples.

The farmers plow in the spring.

1. How many farmers are mentioned in the first sentence? How many in the second? How do you know?
2. Write the plural form of **farmer**.
5. Who owns the trees in the first sentence? How do you know?
6. Write the possessive form of **farmer**.
7. How do the plural and the possessive forms of **farmer** differ?

EXERCISE 1

Write the plural form of each of these nouns.

girl _____   clerk _____   uncle _____

miller _____   cow _____   aunt _____

horse _____   teacher _____   dog _____

sailor _____   cat _____   mouse _____

EXERCISE 2

Write the possessive form of each of these nouns.

girl _____   clerk _____   uncle _____

miller _____   cow _____   aunt _____

horse _____   teacher _____   dog _____

35

EXERCISE 3

In each of the following sentences, supply either the plural or the possessive forms of one of the following nouns.

friend   sailor   rabbit   gorilla

1. Good _____ seldom quarrel.

2. My _____ house was burned last night.

3. What do _____ do for us?

4. A _____ life is full of danger.

5. The _____ face is almost human.

6. _____ are found in Africa.

7. We found a _____ tracks in the snow.

8. They never shoot _____ for sport.

EXERCISE 4

Read each sentence once, then write it from memory on another sheet of paper.

1. Are all the pupils here today?
2. Miss Hunt's poems fill a book.
3. There goes the doctor's horse.
4. Well people need no doctors!

Lesson 19
A POEM TO LEARN

EXERCISE

Copy the following selection onto another sheet of paper. If your teacher asks you to, learn it and recite it.

THE GARDENER

The gardener does not love to talk,
He makes me keep the gravel walk;
And when he puts his tools away
He locks the door and takes the key.

Away behind the currant row,
Where no one else but cook may go,
Far in the plots, I see him dig,
Old and serious, brown and big.

He digs the flowers, green, red and blue,
Nor wishes to be spoken to.
He digs the flowers and cuts the hay,
And never seems to want to play.

Silly gardener! summer goes,
And winter comes with pinching toes,
When in the garden bare and brown
You must lay your barrow down.

Well now, and while the summer stays
To profit by these garden days,
O how much wiser you would be
To play at Indian wars with me!

Robert Louis Stevenson

Lesson 20
PICTURE LESSON: FRANK'S BIRTHDAY PRESENT

EXERCISE

Make up a story from this picture. You might call it "Frank's Birthday Present." Think it over, and then tell it to your teacher.

Lesson 21
PRACTICE IN WRITING QUOTATIONS

"I am a peddler," said Henry.

"What do you sell?" asked Mrs. Ward.

"I sell candy and apples," Henry replied.

"Your candy is good!" exclaimed his mother.

Just what did Henry say in the first sentence?

Tell the exact words his mother said in the second sentence.

When we repeat the exact words of another person, we are said to **quote** them, or make a **quotation**.

Quote Henry's answer to his mother's first question.

1. What quotation do you find in the fourth sentence?
2. With what kind of letter does each quotation begin?
3. Which quotations are statements?
4. With what punctuation mark are the statements separated from the rest of the sentence?
5. Read the quotation that is a question. By what mark is it followed?
6. Read the quotation that is an exclamation. By what mark is it followed?
7. What marks do you observe before each quotation?
8. What marks come after each quotation?

The marks (" ") which enclose quotations are called **quotation marks**.

A quoted sentence must begin with a **capital letter**.

It must be enclosed in **quotation marks** (" ").

It must be set off from the rest of the sentence by a **comma** (,), a **question mark** (?), or an **exclamation mark** (!).

EXERCISE 1

Copy the following quotations, adding the correct punctuation.

1. My eyes are tired said Charles
2. You must have strained them said his father
3. Watch out for that truck the workers shouted
4. These grapes are sour the fox remarked
5. Have your tickets ready called the conductor
6. How many stars are on our flag asked Mr Hayes

1. _____

_____

2. _____

_____

3. _____

_____

4. _____

_____

5. _____

_____

6. _____

_____

EXERCISE 2

Finish the conversation begun between Mrs. Ward and Henry the peddler at the beginning of this lesson. How does he answer his mother? What does she say next? Think about why Henry might be trying to sell candy and apples to his mother.

EXERCISE 3

Read the following sentences. Notice that a comma separates the quotation from the rest of the sentnece.

> Henry said, "I am a peddler."
> Mrs. Ward asked, "What do you sell?"
> Henry replied, "I sell candy and apples."
> His mother exclaimed, "Your candy is good!"

Copy these sentences on another sheet of paper.

EXERCISE 4

Write the following from dictation on another sheet of paper.

1. "Come and speak with me," Mother called.

2. A man who received a dime for rescuing another from drowning said, "Do you think you're worth so little, Sir?"

3. Mrs. Davis asked, "Did you let your sister choose a treat?"

4. "I told her that she might have the little one or none at all," said the selfish boy.

Lesson 22
PRACTICE IN WRITING DIVIDED QUOTATIONS

"Which of you," asked Mr. Brown, "can tell me what a palace is?"
"I think," said Edna, "that a palace is a king's house."

Read the question Mr. Brown asked. Underline the words he actually said.

1. Into how many sections are Mr. Brown's words divided?
2. Tell what words come between the two sections.
3. Circle all quotation marks in the first sentence.
4. Tell which words are between each set of quotation marks.
5. Tell why the words **asked Mr. Brown** are not enclosed in quotation marks.
6. Tell where commas are used in the first sentence.

When a quotation is **divided** into two parts by other words, each part must be enclosed in **quotation marks** (" ") and separated from the rest of the sentence by a **comma** (,).

EXERCISE 1
Copy the following quotations on the lines below.

1. "We shall go if it does not rain," he said. _____

_____

2. "We shall go," he said, "if it does not rain." _____

_____

3. Tom shouted, "Run up the flag, for our side has won!" _____

_____

_____

4. "Run up the flag," Tom shouted, "for our side has won!" _____

_____

_____

5. "If we follow this road, will it take us to the spring?" the hiker asked. _____

_____

_____

6. "If we follow this road," the hiker asked, "will it take us to the spring?" _____

_____

_____

EXERCISE 2
Write the following quotations, inserting correct punctuation.

1. Where called Jane is the candy I left on this table _____

_____

_____

2. My big sister said Joseph just bought a new car _____

_____

_____

3. This time next Friday explained Mattie we leave the city _____

_____

_____

EXERCISE 3

On a separate piece of paper, write these quotations from dictation.

1. "Come again," said he, "when you can stay longer."
2. "Mother," Clara asked, "are the stars angels' eyes ?"
3. "No, my dear," answered her mother, "they are great suns like ours."
4. Bill asked, "How many stars are there?"
5. "How bright the moon is!" Clara said.

Lesson 23
PRACTICE IN WRITING CONVERSATIONS

THE ROBIN'S ADVICE

Down in a field, one day in June,
    The flowers all bloomed together,
Save one who tried to hide herself,
    And drooped, that pleasant weather.

A robin that had flown too high,
    And felt a little lazy,
Was resting near this buttercup,
    Who wished she were a daisy.

For daisies grow so big and tall;
    She always had a passion
For wearing frills about her neck
    In just the daisies' fashion.
And buttercups must always be
    The same old tiresome color,
While daisies dress in gold and white,
    Although their gold is duller.

"Dear Robin," said this sad young flower,
    "Perhaps you'd not mind trying
To find a nice white frill for me,
    Some day when you are flying."

"You silly thing !" the robin said;
    "I think you must be crazy
I'd rather be my honest self
    Than any made-up daisy.

"You're nicer in your own bright gown,
  The little children love you
Be the best buttercup you can,
  And think no flower above you.

"Though swallows leave me out of sight,
  We'd better keep our places;
Perhaps the world would all go wrong
  With one too many daisies.

"Look bravely up into the sky,
  And be content with knowing
That God wished for a buttercup
  Just here where you are growing."

Sarah Orne Jewett

EXERCISE

Suppose the robin in this story met a bluebird on the way home and told him all about the discontented buttercup. On a separate sheet of paper, write what the robin might say to the bluebird.

Lesson 24
NATURE LESSON: THE BALTIMORE ORIOLE

[Ideally, this lesson should be given in the proper season, after actual study of the Baltimore oriole. For background on the oriole read pages 120-123 of Anna Comstock's *Handbook of Nature Study*. Alternatively, you might look up the bird in an encyclopedia. Suggested Internet supplements for this lesson can be found in the Internet Resources appendix.]

Your teacher will either tell you about the Baltimore oriole or show you where you might find information about this bird. Listen or look for answers to the following questions.

1. What are the colors of this bird?
2. For whom is it named?
3. *Oriole* comes from a Latin word meaning *golden*. Tell why this bird called the oriole.
4. What leads us to think it is a tropical bird?
5. How early in the spring do orioles come?
6. In what trees do they build their nests?
7. What is the shape of an oriole's nest?
8. Why is it made so deep?
9. Of what is it made?
10. What does the bird use for a needle in weaving the nest?
11. Which bird does the weaving, the male or the female?
12. For what purpose does a bird build a nest?
13. Which of the pair sits upon the eggs? Which is brighter in color?
14. Why is the bird not easily seen when sitting in the nest?
15. In what season can you find the nests most easily?
16. Which bird is the better singer?
17. Where are orioles in winter?
18. Why do they go away?
19. Upon what do they feed?

EXERCISE 1

Draw a picture of a Baltimore oriole. Draw another picture of an oriole nest. If you keep a nature notebook, you could do this in your notebook.

EXERCISE 2

Write a page or two telling what you have learned about the Baltimore oriole.

Lesson 25
NOUNS MADE PLURAL BY ADDING -ES

Tell your teacher how the plural forms of these words would be made.

      sled   skate   net   monarch

What letter did you add to these words to make them **plural**?

*The following words are made plural by adding **-es**. Add **-es** to the end of each of them, then read each word aloud.*

     glass _____   box _____   dish _____

     church _____   topaz _____

Answer these questions with your teacher.

1. How many syllables are there in the singular forms of these words?
2. How many syllables are in the plural forms?
3. How would these words sound if only **-s** were added?

> **Nouns ending in -s, -x, -z, -sh, or -ch form their plurals by adding -es to the singular.**

EXERCISE 1

Make the following singular nouns plural.

dog _____   bunch _____   apple _____

kiss _____   bush _____   fax _____

fez _____   fox _____

EXERCISE 2

*Without looking back, tell when you should use **-es** to make nouns plural. Write your answer here.*

_____

_____

_____

Lesson 26
MORE PLURAL OR POSSESSIVE NOUNS

Read the following words aloud.

foxes   fox's

Use each word in a sentence.

foxes _____

_____

fox's _____

_____

> Nouns ending in **-s, -x, -z, -sh,** or **-ch** form their **possessive**
> by adding **apostrophe -s ('s)** to the singular.

Since the plural and the possessive forms of these words will sound alike, you will have to listen carefully to how each word is used in a sentence to know how you should write it.

EXERCISE 1
Listen as your teacher reads these sentences. Tell whether the words she names are plural or singular possessive.

1. How many Jameses are in the class?
2. Listen! Was that the fox's bark?
3. Three foxes have been caught.
4. Charles's family name is Mason.

51

EXERCISE 2

Spell first the possessive and then the plural of these words.

grass _____   _____

lass _____   _____

Agnes _____   _____

ostrich _____   _____

bush _____   _____

branch _____   _____

box _____   _____

larch _____   _____

EXERCISE 3

Use the plurals of three of the words from in Exercise 2 in sentences.

1. _____

_____

2. _____

_____

3. _____

EXERCISE 4

On another sheet of paper, write these sentences from dictation.

1. Were there boys in the lady's carriage?
2. Bring Harry's hat and James's coat.
3. I'm glad that you're here.
4. He hears you.
5. Here's enough.
6. Are the churches open on Christmas?

Lesson 27
A POEM TO STUDY

DOING ITS BEST

I am but a tiny cricket,
Living in a summer thicket
    There I take my rest.
Many songs are gayer, prouder;
Many a voice is sweeter, louder,
    But I do my best.

In my song there's no complaining,
Even when the sky is raining;
    Birds fly east and west
Silent hide in leafy cover;
But I chirp till all is over,
    Doing still my best!

EXERCISE 1

Tell your teacher about the poem you just read. Who is the speaker, and what do you learn about him?

EXERCISE 2

Learn these stanzas. Write them from memory on another sheet of paper.

EXERCISE 3

Write the following as six lines of poetry. Indent every other line, beginning with the second. There should be nine capitals.

I would not hurt a living thing, however weak or small; the beasts that graze, the birds that sing, our father made them all; without his notice, I have read, a sparrow cannot fall.

Lesson 28
SYNONYMS

You have learned about **homonyms**, words that have the same sounds but different meanings. There are also many words that do not sound at all alike, but have similar meanings. These words are called **synonyms**.

If you wanted to say that someone is **pleasant to look at**, you might call that person **pretty, handsome** or **beautiful**. If you wanted to say that a boy **moved quickly**, you might say that he **ran** or **raced, bolted,** or **loped**.

Words that have nearly the same meaning are called synonyms.

EXERCISE 1
How many synonyms can you think of for each of the following words?

laugh _____

_____

friend _____

_____

said _____

_____

boy _____

_____

bite _____

_____

EXERCISE 2

Choose one of the lists of words you made in Exercise 1 and write a sentence for each of the synonyms you listed.

1. _____

_____

2. _____

_____

3. _____

_____

4. _____

_____

5. _____

_____

6. _____

_____

7. _____

_____

Lesson 29
CHOOSING THE BEST WORD

Perhaps you have made a hop-skip-and-jump or watched others make it. What is the difference between the **hop** and the **skip**? Between the **hop** and the **jump**? Between the **skip** and the **jump**? Could you say a **hop-jump-and-leap**? What is the difference between a **jump** and a **leap**? If a cannon went off behind you unexpectedly, would you **jump** or **leap**?

When a visitor comes into a room, you may **look**, but you must not **stare**. What is the difference between **looking** and **staring**?

Watch the leaves of different trees when the wind is blowing through them. Some leaves **shake**, some **tremble**, some **quiver**. What is the difference?

If you should go out in a cold wind without your coat, would you **shake**, **shiver**, or **quiver**? What is the difference?

EXERCISE 1
Answer the following questions with your teacher.

What would be the best word for these sentences?

       The queen _____ her soup.

       The starving dog _____ his food.

In which of the following sentences would you use the word **horse**? In which the word **steed**?

       Dr. Carson rides an old gray _____ .

       The warrior mounted his fiery _____ .

EXERCISE 2

Answer the following questions with your teacher.

A man who is carrying two bundles under his arm drops both of them on the sidewalk.
One of them falls with a **crash**, the other with a **clatter**.
What might be in each bundle?

What do you do when you **throw** a stone? What do you do when you **fling** it?

Is a fox who steals a chicken out of a guarded hen house **bold** or **brave**?
Can you think of any wild animal that is brave?
What might a dog do to show that he is brave?

Does **dancing** call up a picture different from **capering**?
Does **smooth** call up a picture different from **slippery**?
Does **walking** call up a picture different from **striding**?
Does **strikes** call up a picture different from **pounds**?
What is the difference in each case?

EXERCISE 3

What pictures do you imagine as you read the following?

The children are dancing on the lawn.
The children are capering on the lawn.

The ice on the pond is smooth.
The ice on the pond is slippery.

John is walking down the street.
John is striding down the street.

When dinner is ready, a waiter comes to the front door
and strikes the gong.
When dinner is ready, a waiter comes to the front door
and pounds on the gong.

Lesson 30
REVIEW

EXERCISE 1

1. *Write a statement about a fish.* _____

_____

_____

2. *Change the statement to a question.* _____

_____

_____

3. *Which words are always begun with capitals?* _____

_____

_____

4. *Think of a word pronounced like the word* **vain**.

a. *Write it and tell its meaning.* _____

_____

b. *Write a statement that tells something that you know about it.* _____

_____

5. Ask a question about the weather yesterday and another about the weather tomorrow. Use a contraction in each sentence.

a. _____

_____

_____

b. _____

_____

EXERCISE 2

1. What is the difference between a **contraction** and an **abbreviation**? _____

_____

_____

2. Write a statement telling where a friend of yours lives. _____

_____

_____

3. Write another friend's name, and the name of the street, town, and state where your friend lives. Use proper abbreviations.

_____

_____

4. *Write a statement about a house in your neighborhood.*
Use the possessive form of the owner's name.

_____

_____

_____

5. *Rewrite this sentence, using the possessive of* **Mr. Curtis**.

He is the son of Mr. Curtis.

_____

6. *In one sentence, tell something you saw from your window this morning.*
Begin the sentence with the word **There's**.

_____

_____

7. *Write a question about something in the school room.*
Begin the sentence with the words **Is there**.

_____

_____

_____

EXERCISE 3

1. *Write a sentence beginning with* **Yesterday my father said to me.**
   Use quotation marks correctly.

   _____

   _____

   _____

2. *Use the contraction for* **are not** *in a sentence about pigeons.* _____

   _____

   _____

3. *In a single sentence, tell what happened yesterday afternoon. Use* **PM** *and a date.*

   _____

   _____

   _____

4. *Write a sentence beginning with* **At the beginning of my lesson the teacher asked me.**
   Quote the words of the teacher. Punctuate the sentence correctly.

   _____

   _____

   _____

Lesson 31
PICTURE LESSON: AMUSING A CHILD

Both of the older children in the picture are eager to play with their little brother. "Very well," says the mother, "I will let each one of you try to amuse him for a quarter of an hour by the clock. What will you do to keep him happy?" Each sister tells her mother what she will do.

1. What time is it according to the clock at the top of the picture?
2. A quarter of an hour is how many minutes?
3. Where will the hands of the clock be at the end of the first quarter?
4. Where will they be at the end of the second quarter?
5. Think about what you might do to keep the baby happy if you were one of the girls. Can you imagine what each child might say?
6. Tell first what the little one will do, then tell what the older sister will do.

EXERCISE

On another sheet of paper, write a story about what happens as the two sisters (or a brother and a sister or two brothers) play with their little brother.

Lesson 32
PLURAL POSSESSIVE NOUNS

Read the following words.

lady	clerk	tailor	bird
lady's	clerk's	tailor's	bird's

Circle the words which speak of **only one**.
Underline the words which mean **belonging to only one**.

Tell your teacher how **'s** (**apostrophe -s**) changes the meaning of each word.
For what is **'s** used?

Read these words.

ladies	clerks	tailors	birds
ladies'	clerks'	tailors'	birds'

Circle the words which speak of **more than one**.
Underline the words which mean **belonging to more than one**.

Where do you find the apostrophe in these words?
For what is it used?

Plural nouns ending in -s are made possessive by adding the apostrophe (') after the final -s.

For example: frogs'.

Read the following sentences.

The store belonging to my brother is closed.
My brother's store is closed.

The store belonging to my brothers is open.
My brothers' store is open.

1. In the first two sentences, how many brothers own the store?
2. In the next two sentences, how many brothers own the store?
3. Tell your teacher the difference between **brother's** and **brothers'**.
   Both are possessive, but which is singular and which is plural?

EXERCISE 1
Circle the objects that have more than one owner.

my uncle's boat	the girls' sled	the bird's nest
my uncles' boat	the girl's sled	the birds' nest

EXERCISE 2
Tell whether these nouns are singular or plural. How do you know?

lady's	merchants'	lions'
merchant's	baker's	sons'
crow's	bakers'	swans'
farmer's	ladies'	

EXERCISE 3
Complete the following on a separate piece of paper:
Write three sentences using five plural possessive nouns.
Write three sentences using five plural nouns.
Write two sentences using two singular possessive nouns.

Lesson 33
STORIES TO NARRATE

EXERCISE 1

Read this story silently, then tell it to your teacher from memory.

Patty received a doll's trunk at Christmas. As Paula seemed to wish for one, their grandmother (who acted as "fairy godmother" to the children) gave her one for her birthday. Paula's trunk happened to be a little smaller than Patty's, and Patty liked nothing better than to call Paula's attention to this fact.

Paula bore it very well, until the day when Patty said with a pitying air, "Paula, I'm so used to my big trunk that when I look at yours it seems small to me!"

Paula turned quickly to say, "Well, I don't care, Patty. You're not a bit nice! It isn't the smallness you ought to look at when someone gives you something, it's the kindness!"

EXERCISE 2

Read the following story silently, then write it from memory. Be careful to punctuate it correctly.

An English minister once said to a bright little girl in his Sunday School, "If you will tell me where God is, I will give you an orange."

"If you will tell me where He is not," promptly replied the little girl, "I will give you two."

EXERCISE 3

*Find some good short story or anecdote, and tell it to your teacher in your own words. Do not use **and** very often.*

Lesson 34
NATURE LESSON: BARN SWALLOWS

[Like the earlier lesson about the Balimore oriole, this lesson should ideally be given in the proper season, after an actual study of the barn swallow. For background information on the barn swallow, see pages 109-115 of Comstock's *Handbook of Nature Study*. Suggested Internet supplements for this lesson can be found in the Internet Resources appendix.]

Your teacher will either tell you about the barn swallow or show you where you might find information about this bird. Listen or look for answers to the following questions.

1. What does this bird look like? Describe its color and its markings.
2. Describe the shape of its beak, and tell how this design is useful to the bird.
3. Where do barn swallows build their nests?
4. Describe the nest's shape.
5. Of what is the nest made?
6. What time of year do we see barn swallows?
7. Where do barn swallows spend the winter months?
8. What do barn swallows eat?
9. How are barn swallows useful to us?

EXERCISE 1
Draw a picture of a barn swallow. Draw a picture of barn swallow's nest. If you keep a nature notebook, you may draw your pictures in it.

EXERCISE 2
Write a page or two telling what you have learned about the barn swallow.

EXERCISE 3
An oriole explains to a barn swallow how a nest should be built. He does not like the barn swallow's style of house and thinks his own is much better. He calls attention to its advantages in different kinds of weather. What do the two birds say to one another? On a separate piece of paper, write out their conversation, being careful to punctuate it correctly.

Lesson 35
A POEM TO COPY

EXERCISE

Copy the following selection onto a separate piece of paper.

They'll come again to the apple-tree,
Robin and all the rest,
When the orchard branches are fair to see,
In the snow of the blossoms dressed,
And the prettiest thing in the world will be
The building of the nest.

Author Unknown

Lesson 36
PRACTICE IN USING **WHO'S** AND **WHOSE**

Who's and **whose** are **homonyms**.

Tell your teacher why that is so:

(**Who's** and **whose** _____ alike, but _____ different things.)

Who's is a contraction of **who is**.

> **Who is** going to the river today?
> **Who's** going to the river today?

Whose asks to whom a thing belongs.

> **To whom** does this apron belong?
> **Whose** apron is this?

EXERCISE 1
Choose the correct word for each sentence. Tell why you choose as you do.

> Do you know (who's / whose) **playing at first base?**
> (Who's / Whose) **turn is it to go to bat?**
> (Who's / Whose) **house is that on the hill?**
> (Who's / Whose) **the owner of that house?**
> Tell me (who's / whose) **singing you like best.**
> Tell me (who's / whose) **waiting at the station.**

EXERCISE 2
*On another sheet of paper, write three sentences using **whose**, and three using **who's**.*
Write one sentence using both words. Begin each sentence differently.

Lesson 37
PRACTICE IN USING COMMAS IN A SERIES

Read the following sentences.

Grocers sell tea, sugar, rice, and flour.
Farmers plow, plant, and reap.
Men, women, and children make the nation.

Tell your teacher what is described in the first sentence. What do tea, sugar, rice and flour have in common?

In a sentence, three or more words of the same kind make a **series**.

---

1. Tell your teacher which series of words shows what farmers do.
2. What series is found in the third sentence? How are these words alike?
3. What mark separates each item in the series?

The words of a series are kept separate by **commas**.

EXERCISE

Write answers to each of the following, using a series of words in each sentence. Be sure to punctuate your sentences correctly.

1. What four things might you do in school? _____

_____

2. What can you buy at a furniture store? _____

3. What does the carpenter build? _____

_____

_____

4. What tools does a carpenter use? _____

_____

_____

5. Of what materials may a house be made? _____

_____

_____

6. Which colors are called the *primary colors*? _____

_____

7. What are the *cardinal*, or main, points of the compass? _____

_____

8. What things does a gardener do? _____

_____

_____

_____

Lesson 38
PLURAL POSSESSIVE NOUNS REVIEW

EXERCISE

Write the following from dictation. Your teacher will tell you whether the possessive noun should be plural or singular.

1. **My sisters'** (more than one sister) **birthdays come in October.**
2. **That old soldier's** (one soldier) **stories are interesting.**
3. **My friends'** (more than one friend) **horses are all beautiful.**
4. **The babies'** (more than one baby) **mothers sat on the porch.**
5. **The hero's** (one hero) **family welcomed him home.**

Lesson 39
PLURAL NOUNS ENDING IN -IES

The letters **a**, **e**, **i**, **o**, **u**, and sometimes **y**, are called **vowels**. The other letters of the alphabet are called **consonants**.

Look at the following words. Circle the letter that comes before the -y in each of them.

day	ray	key	valley
boy	toy	guy	

Tell your teacher whether the letters you have circled are consonants or vowels.

> ## Words ending in -y after a **vowel** are made plural by adding -s.

The plurals of these words are spelled like this:

days	rays	keys	valleys
boys	toys	guys	

Look at these words. Circle the letter that comes before the -y.

ruby	lady	fly	story	duty

Tell your teacher whether the letters you have circled are consonants or vowels.

> ## Words ending in -y after a **consonant** are made plural by changing the -y to -i and adding -es.

The plurals of these words are spelled like this:

rubies   ladies   flies   stories   duties

EXERCISE 1
Write the plurals of these words by changing -y to -ies.

berry_____   lily_____   fairy_____

city_____   lady_____   pony_____

enemy_____   sty_____   ditty_____

story_____   cherry_____   cry_____

body_____   jelly_____   dairy_____

daisy_____   tidy_____   reply_____

fly_____   duty_____

EXERCISE 2
Use the plurals of five of the above words in sentences.

1. _____

_____

2. _____

_____

3. _____

4. _____

_____

5. _____

_____

EXERCISE 3

Write these sentences on another sheet of paper as your teacher dictates them to you.

1. "Did you thank Mrs. Lane for the cherries, Alice?" asked Mother.
2. Do such lilies grow in the valleys?
3. The tallest chimneys are in cities.
4. Who's going to eat these berries?
5. The rabbits' homes are covered with small rocks, sticks, and leaves.
6. "The city's enemies will attack us at dawn!" shouted the scout.
7. The ants spoiled the ladies' picnic.
8. Mary asked, "Whose book of stories is this?"

Lesson 40
PICTURE LESSON: THE SOLDIER AND THE BEAR

Study the picture. Talk with your teacher about what you see.

Who do you see in the picture? What do you suppose the men are talking about? How do you think the soldier might have gotten the bear? What name would you give him? What kind of men do these two appear to be? Where are they now? Where do you think they are going?

EXERCISE
Write a story about this picture.

Lesson 41
THERE, THEIR, AND THEY'RE

These homonyms are often confused: **there**, **their**, and **they're**.

There means **in that place.**

> **Put that book there, not here.**

Their means **belonging to them.**

> **That is their book.**

They're is a contraction made up the words **they** and **are**, and so is used in place of **they are**.

> **They're taking the book and leaving.**

EXERCISE 1
*Without looking at your book, tell your teacher how **there**, **their**, and **they're** are spelled, and the differences in their meanings.*

EXERCISE 2
Select the correct one of the three words to supply in each of the following sentences.

1. **Have you moved** _____ **books?**

2. **Let them stay** _____ .

3. _____ **they go with** _____ **dogs!**

4. _____ expecting you _____ today.

5. When were you _____ last?

6. _____ living _____ now with _____ friends.

EXERCISE 3

*To show the proper use of **there**, **their**, and **they're**, write six sentences.*
Write two sentences for each word.

1. _____

_____

2. _____

_____

3. _____

_____

4. _____

_____

5. _____

_____

6. _____

_____

EXERCISE 4

On another sheet of paper, write these sentences as your teacher dictates them to you.

1. John asked, "Are there any apples left?"
2. "Yes," mother said, "here is an apple for you."
3. They're to take their children to the circus today.
4. "There is my lost book!" cried the boy.
5. They should not cry if they've done their best.
6. They're glad you came.

Lesson 42
MORE PRACTICE IN WRITING CONVERSATIONS

You have learned that the sentences in a paragraph should all talk about the same subject. When we begin to talk about a new subject, we should begin a new paragraph. Read the following story and notice where the writer begins each new paragraph.

When I was a boy at school, I was often very idle. Even while at my lessons, I used to play with other boys as idle as myself. Of course we tried to hide this from the teacher, but one day we were caught.

"Boys," he said, "you must not be idle. You must keep your eyes on your lessons. You do not know what you lose by being idle. Now, while you are young, is the time to learn. Let any one of you who sees another boy looking away from his book come and tell me."

"Now," I said to myself after a short time, "there is Fred Smith. I do not like him. I will watch him, and if I see him looking around, I will tell." Not very long after that, I saw Fred looking off his book, so I went up and told the teacher.

"Aha!" he said, "how do you know he was idle?"

"Please, Sir," said I, "I saw him."

"Oh you did, did you? And where were your eyes when you saw him? Were they on your book?"

I was fairly caught. I saw the other boys laugh, and I hung my head while the teacher smiled. It was a good lesson for me. I did not watch for idle boys again.

EXERCISE 1

Get a blue and a red colored pencil. With the red pencil, underline the words the teacher in the story says. Underline the words the boy (or the I) says with the blue pencil. Did you notice that a new paragraph starts every time the speaker changes?

When writing conversation, begin a new paragraph each time the speaker changes.

EXERCISE 2

Write this conversation with correct paragraph divisions.

Once a fox found a bumblebee. He put it into his bag and traveled on. Soon he came to a house. He went in and said to the woman, "May I leave my bag here for awhile?" "Yes, you may," said the woman. "Then be careful not to open the bag," said the fox. As soon as the fox left, the woman opened the bag. The bee flew out, and the rooster ate it. When the fox returned he saw the bee was gone. "Where is my bumble bee?" he said. "Oh, I just untied the bag," said the woman, "and the bee flew out. My rooster ate him." "Very well, then, I must have the rooster," said the fox.

EXERCISE 3

On another sheet of paper, write a conversation between you and a younger child.

Lesson 43
FOURTEEN PLURAL NOUNS ENDING IN -VES

Most nouns ending in **-f** or **-fe** simply add **-s** to form their plurals.

grief	**reef**	**fife**	**strife**
griefs	**reefs**	**fifes**	**strifes**

Fourteen common nouns ending in **-f** or **-fe** form their plurals by changing the **-f** or **-fe** to **-ves**.

calf	**elf**	**half**	**knife**	**leaf**
calves	**elves**	**halves**	**knives**	**leaves**

life	**loaf**	**self**	**sheaf**	**shelf**
lives	**loaves**	**selves**	**sheaves**	**shelves**

staff	**thief**	**wharf**	**wolf**
staves	**thieves**	**wharves**	**wolves**

EXERCISE 1

Working through one pair of words at a time, underline the -f or the -fe in the singular nouns above. Then underline the -ves in the plural form of the same word. The first four have been done for you.

EXERCISE 2

Memorize the first seven words, using the following steps to learn each one.
1. Spell the word aloud as you look at the letters.
2. Copy the word, naming each letter as you write.
3. Close your eyes and picture the word
4. Cover the word and write it from memory, naming each letter as you write.
5. Check yourself.

calf   _____   _____

calves   _____   _____

elf   _____   _____

elves   _____   _____

half   _____   _____

halves   _____   _____

knife   _____   _____

knives   _____   _____

leaf   _____   _____

leaves   _____   _____

life   _____   _____

lives   _____   _____

loaf   _____   _____

loaves   _____   _____

EXERCISE 3

Write seven sentences, using each of the word pairs from Exercise 2.

1. _____

   _____

2. _____

   _____

3. _____

   _____

4. _____

   _____

5. _____

   _____

6. _____

   _____

7. _____

   _____

EXERCISE 4

Repeat exercise 2 with the remaining set of seven words.

self   _____   _____

selves   _____   _____

sheaf   _____   _____

sheaves   _____   _____

shelf   _____   _____

shelves   _____   _____

staff   _____   _____

staves   _____   _____

thief   _____   _____

thieves   _____   _____

wharf   _____   _____

wharves   _____   _____

wolf   _____   _____

wolves   _____   _____

EXERCISE 5

Write seven sentences, using each of the word pairs from Exercise 4.

1. _____

_____

2. _____

_____

3. _____

_____

4. _____

_____

5. _____

_____

6. _____

_____

7. _____

_____

Lesson 44
NATURE LESSON: THE RABBIT'S HOME

[Refer to Anna Comstock's *Handbook of Nature Study*, pages 215-219. Suggested Internet supplements for this lesson can be found in the Internet Resources appendix.]

Answer these questions.

1. In what sort of home does the rabbit live?
2. How is it made?
3. How is it like your home?
4. How is it different? What is the door? What is the roof? How is it kept warm?

EXERCISE

The mother rabbit tells one of the little rabbits how their home was made and how it is different from the homes of people. On another sheet of paper, write what she says to them.

Lesson 45
A POEM TO READ ALOUD

When you read a poem aloud, be sure to pay attention to the punctuation at the ends of lines. Pause at the end of lines ending with commas, just as you would pause for a comma in your other reading. When a line ends in a period, you should stop as you would normally stop for a period.

If there is no punctuation at the end of a line, you may emphasize the last word in that line with your voice, but continue on to the next line without pausing. You should always read a poem with a natural tone and avoid falling into a sing-song-like rhythm.

Practice reading this poem aloud.

Among the sand-hills
    Near by the sea,
Wild young rabbits
    Were seen by me.

They live in borrows
    With winding ways,
And there they shelter
    On rainy days.

The mother rabbits
    Make cozy nests,
With hairy linings
    From their breasts.

The tender young ones
    Are nursed and fed,
And safely hidden
    In this warm bed.

And when they are older,
    They all come out
Upon the sand-hills,
    And frisk about.

They play and nibble
    The long, dry grass,
But scamper away
    Whenever you pass.

Author unknown

EXERCISE

If your teacher would like you to do so, memorize this poem and recite it.

Lesson 46
WRITING THE TITLES OF LONG WORKS

Read the following sentences.

I am sure you will enjoy <u>Robinson Crusoe</u>.

My father likes to read <u>World Magazine</u>.

Our city's main newspaper is *The Whoville Gazette*.

If you wish to write the title of a book, newspaper, magazine, or other book length work, you should either **underline** or **italicize** the title.

Notice how the titles of books are written in the following sentences.

Sally told me she has finished <u>Tame Animals I Have Known</u>.

Joe's favorite book is *The Wind in the Willows*.

Have you ever read <u>The Horse and His Boy</u>?

[Note to teacher: When typing on a computer, it is acceptable to either underline or italicize the title of any book length work (including titles of periodicals, newspapers, pamphlets, plays, films, long poems, long musical compositions, telelvision and radio shows, and works of visual art), although there is a preference for the use of italics. If you are writing a book title by hand (or using the now almost extinct typewriter), it is best to underline it.]

Answer the following questions with your teacher.

1. Do all the words in the previously mentioned titles begin with capital letters?
2. Which words do begin with capitals?
3. Which words do not?

The titles of books,
          magazines, newspapers, and other periodicals,
          long poems,
          pamphlets,
          plays and films,
          long musical compositions,
          telelvision and radio shows, and
          works of visual art

are **underlined** **when** handwritten and ***italicized*** when typed.

EXERCISE

Answer the following questions on another sheet of paper, writing in complete sentences.

1. What is the name of the last book you read?
2. What is the title of your math book?
3. What is the title of your favorite book?
4. What is the largest book you have ever seen?
5. What is the title of the longest book you have ever read?

The principal words in the titles of books or book length works should begin with **capital letters**.

The first word of a title always begins with a **capital letter**.

Lesson 47
WRITING THE TITLES OF SHORT WORKS

Read the following sentences to your teacher.

Last year we memorized the poem "Ozymandias."

Did you read the article "Birds in Winter" in your last <u>Nature Magazine</u>?

My favorite song is "Sweet Betsy from Pike."

"Ozymandias," "Birds in Winter," and "Sweet Betsy from Pike" are titles of what kinds of things?

1. "Ozymandias" is a _____ .

2. "Birds in Winter" is an _____ .

3. "Sweet Betsy from Pike" is a _____ .

Poems, magazine or newspaper articles, and other short works are not long enough to be published individually. They are usually part of larger works.

The titles of magazine and newspaper articles,
        short poems,
        short stories, and
        short musical compositions
are written inside **quotation marks** (" ").

EXERCISE

Write the titles of two songs you like.

_____

1.

_____

2.

Write the titles of two poems you have learned.

_____

1.

_____

2.

Write the titles of two newspaper or magazine articles you have read this week.

_____

1.

_____

2.

Lesson 48
COPY WORK

EXERCISE

Copy these three pieces of advice neatly onto another sheet of paper. Tell your teacher what each means. What do you think of the advice given?

Work while you work and play while you play.
That is the way to be cheerful each day.

All that you do, do with all your might.
Things done by halves are never done right.

Joy and temperance and repose
Slam the door on the doctor's nose.

Lesson 49
DICTATION REVIEW

EXERCISE

Write these sentences from dictation on another sheet of paper.

1. The rabbits' homes are covered with small rocks, sticks, and leaves.
2. "The wolves are coming!" shouted the boy.
3. "When they come," said the man, "we'll be ready."
4. The men spoiled the wolves' dinner plans.
5. The girls put the dolls on the shelves and changed the dolls' beds.
6. Fred asked, "Whose knife is this?"

Lesson 50
PICTURE LESSON: HELPING MOTHER

Study this picture. Who and what do you see? What are the girls helping their mother make? Describe the room in which they are working.

EXERCISE
Write a story about these girls and their mother. Tell who they are and what they did one day.

Lesson 51
PRACTICE IN WRITING FRIENDLY LETTERS

Read the following letter.

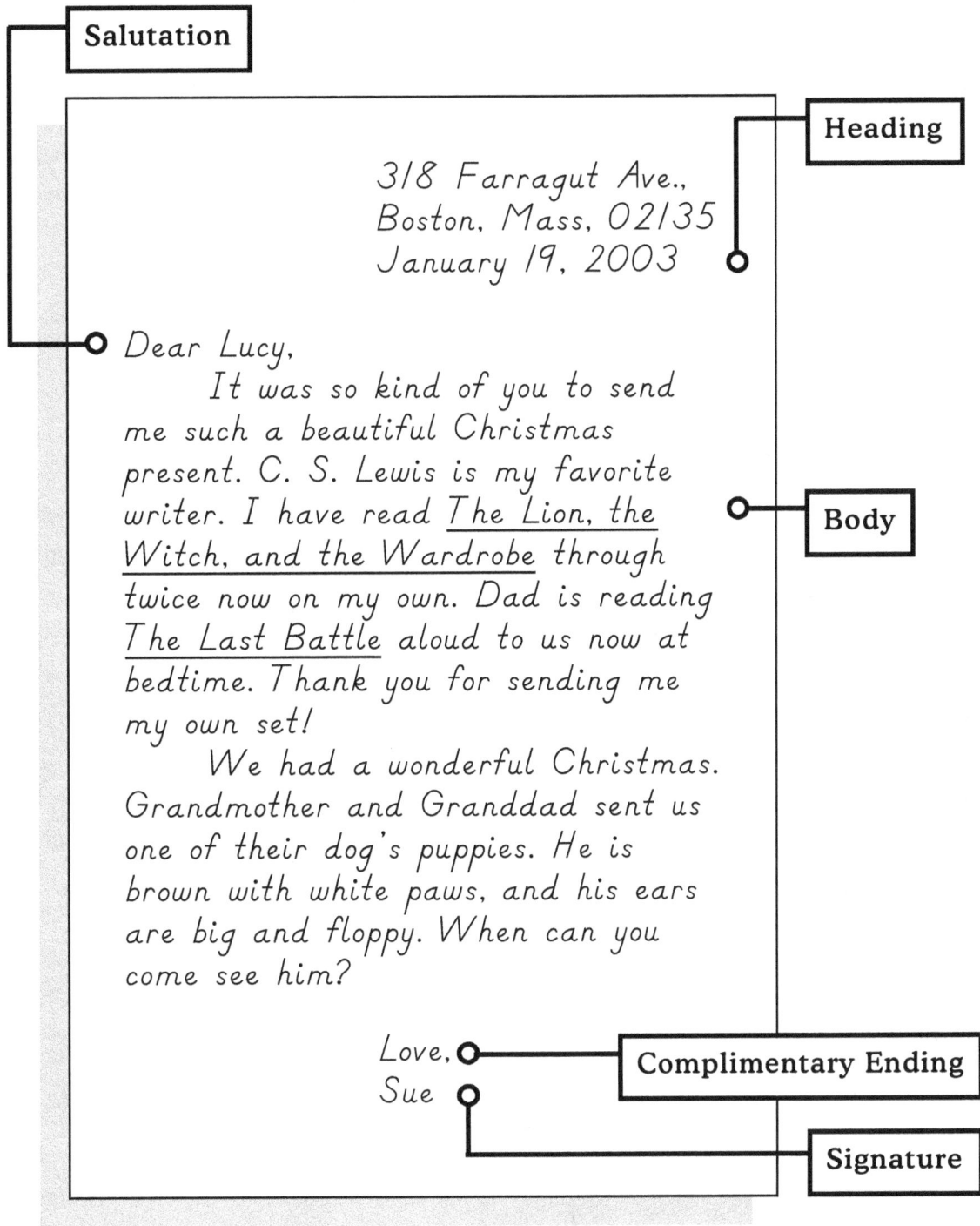

Salutation

Heading

318 Farragut Ave.,
Boston, Mass, 02135
January 19, 2003

Dear Lucy,
    It was so kind of you to send
me such a beautiful Christmas
present. C. S. Lewis is my favorite
writer. I have read <u>The Lion, the
Witch, and the Wardrobe</u> through
twice now on my own. Dad is reading
<u>The Last Battle</u> aloud to us now at
bedtime. Thank you for sending me
my own set!
    We had a wonderful Christmas.
Grandmother and Granddad sent us
one of their dog's puppies. He is
brown with white paws, and his ears
are big and floppy. When can you
come see him?

Body

Love,
Sue

Complimentary Ending

Signature

THE HEADING

The first part, or **heading**, of a letter should show the address of the writer and the date the letter was written.

The first line should show the **street address**.

The second line should show the **city** or **town**, the **state**, and the **zip code**.

The third line should showhe **date** the letter is written.

THE SALUTATION

The second part of the letter is called the **salutation**. The salutation is made up of a pleasant greeting and the name of the person to whom you are writing.

Tell your teacher what two words make up the salutation in Sue's letter.

THE BODY

On the next line the main part, or **body**, of the letter begins. Each paragraph should be correctly indented.

Tell your teacher how many paragraphs make up the body of Sue's letter.

THE COMPLIMENTARY ENDING

After the body of the letter comes some kindly or courteous expression that shows the feeling of the writer towards the one who receives the letter. This is called the **complimentary ending**, or the **conclusion**. Nothing else should be written on the same line with the conclusion, and a comma should be written at the end of this line.

Tell your teacher how Sue concludes her letter.

THE SIGNATURE

Last of all is the **signature** of the writer. Because Sue knows Lucy well, she signs with only her nickname, **Sue**. If she did not know Lucy very well, how do you think she might sign her name?

EXERCISE

On another sheet of paper, copy Sue's letter to Lucy. Use your address and today's date for the heading of your copy.

Lesson 52
PRACTICE IN ADDRESSING ENVELOPES

```
Susan Green
318 Farragut Ave.
Boston, MA 02135


                    Miss Lucy Jones
                    3442 Stratford Rd.
                    Atlanta, Ga. 30327
```

The address on an envelope should always be carefully written.

The proper title* should be used with the name on the first line. The street name and the house or apartment number should be clearly written on the second line. The name of the city or town, the state, and the zip code are written on the third line.

EXERCISE

Address an envelope as you would address it if you were sending a letter to Sue.

* The most common proper titles are **Mr.**, **Mrs.**, **Miss**, **Ms.**, and **Dr.**

Lesson 53
A LETTER TO WRITE

Imagine that you are this little girl writing a letter to her grandmother. She has gotten out paper, a pen, and an ink bottle. Where did she find these things? Is she allowed to use the pen and ink? She has tried to write at the table, but it is too high for her. How did the kitten try to help? What will the little girl tell her grandmother about the kitten and the ink spill?

EXERCISE
Write a letter to a relative or a friend who does not live near you. Address the envelope correctly and ask your teacher or your parents to mail it for you.

Lesson 54
IRREGULAR PLURAL NOUNS

*Tell your teacher how you would speak of **more than one** of each of the following nouns.*

one man, two _____   one goose, two _____

one tooth, two _____   one ox, two _____

one mouse, two _____   one woman, two _____

one foot, two _____   one child, two _____

Some nouns form their plurals in irregular ways. No **-s** is added; instead, another form of the word is used. For example: **man** becomes **men**, **child** becomes **children**.

Sometimes the same word is used for both the singular and the plural.

Read these sentences aloud with your teacher.

> **The farmer counted his sheep.**
> **One sheep was missing.**

> **There are five deer in the park.**
> **Have you ever seen a wild deer?**

In the first two sentences, which word speaks of **one sheep**?
Which speaks of **more than one sheep**?

In the third and fourth sentences, which word speaks of **one deer**?
Which speaks of **more than one deer**?

Some words have the same form in the singular and the plural.
For example: **sheep, deer, trout, cannon,** and **fish.**

EXERCISE

Write sentences containing the plural forms of these words.

1. woman _____

_____

_____

2. ox _____

_____

_____

3. man _____

_____

_____

4. foot _____

_____

_____

5. child _____

_____

_____

6. tooth _____

_____

7. mouse _____

_____

_____

8. goose _____

_____

_____

9. fish _____

_____

_____

10. cannon _____

_____

_____

11. sheep _____

_____

_____

Lesson 55
MAKING IRREGULAR PLURAL NOUNS POSSESSIVE

Read the following sentences with your teacher.

Men's voices were heard.
Did you see the children's presents?

Answer these questions with your teacher.

1. In the first sentence, whose voices are heard? Does the sentence speak of one voice or more than one voice?
2. In the second sentence, are there presents for one child, or for more than one child?
3. What has been added to **men** and to **children** to show that the men and the children possess something?

To form the possessive of a **plural** noun not ending in **-s**, add an **apostrophe** (') and **-s**.

EXERCISE 1
From the list of possessive nouns below, circle the nouns that speak of **more than one**. Underline the word which could speak of either **one** or **more than one**.

boy's	sister's	teachers'	men's
boys'	women's	girls'	man's
bee's	ladies'	fish's	

EXERCISE 2
Write four forms (**singular**, **singular possessive**, **plural**, and **plural possessive**) of each of the nouns below.

friend _____ _____ _____ _____

father _____ _____ _____ _____

sailor _____ _____ _____ _____

mother _____ _____ _____ _____

child _____ _____ _____ _____

gentleman _____ _____

_____ _____

Lesson 56
NATURE LESSON: THE HARVEST MOUSE

[Suggested Internet supplements for this lesson can be found in the Internet Resources appendix.]

BABIES THAT LIVE IN A BALL

In this picture you see the home of the babies that live in a ball. This little ball was built on stalks of wheat by an animal called the harvest mouse.

The ball is not much larger than an egg, and yet there are sometimes three or four little harvest mice in it. They are baby harvest mice. Of course, they must be very small to live in such a little house. The mother of these little harvest mice is not half so large as the little mouse you might see running about in a barn or a house. This little mouse is almost red on her back. The under part of her body is soft and white like silk, and her ears are short.

Even wise men do not know how so small an animal can make this pretty ball. We cannot tell how she fastens the ball to the wheat stalks, nor how she gets into it to feed the baby mice.

In the picture you see the mother harvest mouse sitting on the nest, eating her dinner. She has a little bug for her dinner. Father Mouse is away, trying to find one for his dinner. Do you see his tail curled around the wheat stalk? The tail of the harvest mouse is as long as his whole body, and he can hold on with it as if it were a hand.

The little harvest mice do not spend their winters in this airy home. They make a snug, warm house under the ground. In this winter house is a room large enough for all the harvest mice; but even so, their winter house still seems very small to us.

EXERCISE 1

Tell what you have learned about the harvest mouse.

EXERCISE 2

On another sheet of paper, draw a picture of the mouse and write a paragraph describing the creature. If you keep a nature notebook, put your picture and description in it.

Lesson 57
A POEM TO LEARN

EXERCISE

Copy the following selection onto another sheet of paper. If your teacher asks you to, learn it and recite it.

> If little things that God has made,
> > Are useful in their kind,
> O let us learn a simple truth,
> And bear it on our mind:
> That every child can praise Him,
> > However weak and small;
> Let each with joy remember this,
> > That God has work for all.

Author unknown

Lesson 58
REVIEW OF PLURAL NOUNS

1. When is a word said to be in the singular form?
2. When is a word said to be in the plural form?
3. How are the plural forms of most nouns made?
4. Name five nouns that form their plurals by adding **-s** to the singular.
5. How do some nouns ending in a hissing sound, like **-s**, **-x**, **-sh**, and **-ch**, form their plurals? Give the plural forms of five nouns ending in **-s**, **-x**, **-sh**, or **-ch**.
6. How do some nouns ending in **-f** or **-fe** form their plurals? Give examples.
7. In how many ways can nouns ending in **-y** form their plurals? Give examples of each way, and tell how the plural is formed in each case.
8. Name five nouns that form their plurals irregularly.
9. Name three nouns for which the singular and the plural forms are the same.

EXERCISE 1
Write the plural form of each noun in the spaces below.

basket _____   turkey _____   dish _____

story _____   leaf _____   woman _____

fish _____

EXERCISE 2
Write statements containing the plural forms of these words.

1. ox _____

_____

2. family _____

3. city _____

_____

EXERCISE 3

Write questions using the plural forms of these words.

1. knife _____

_____

2. journey _____

_____

3. sheep _____

_____

EXERCISE 4

Write commands using the plural forms of these words.

1. pony _____

_____

2. match _____

_____

3. child _____

Lesson 59
DICTATION REVIEW

EXERCISE

Write these sentences from dictation on another sheet of paper.

1. Butterflies have short lives.
2. "The thieves escaped in an old brown truck," said the sheriff.
3. The chimneys of three cities can be seen from this hill.
4. Monkeys, parrots, and big snakes are found in the forests of Central America.
5. The hills and valleys are bright with autumn leaves.
6. Whose sand pail was left there by the sea?
7. The dogs' dishes need to be washed.
8. The children's toys were left in the yard.

Lesson 60
PICTURE LESSON: A HEAVY LOAD

Perhaps these children are enjoying the first day of their summer vacation. What names would you give them? Where do you suppose they are going? From what place did they set out? How do you think they will spend their afternoon? How would you like to spend the first day of your summer vacation?

EXERCISE

When the children return home, the girl in the basket will tell all about the day's adventure. Tell the story of their day.

Appendix:
Internet Resources for
Selected Nature Lessons

LESSON 12: BUTTERFLIES
www.enchantedlearning.com/subjects/butterfly/
This is a very nice site. It contains basic information, printouts, and life cycles.

www.hhmi.org/coolscience/butterfly/
This is an art project on the life cycle of a butterfly.

www.butterflywebsite.com/sponsors/sponsordisplay.cfm?product=livebutterflies
This is a list of sources for live butterflies and butterfly kits.

LESSON 24: BALTIMORE ORIOLES
www.mbr-pwrc.usgs.gov/id/framlst/i5070id.html

www.enchantedlearning.com/subjects/birds/printouts/Orioleprintout.shtml

LESSON 34: BARN SWALLOWS
www.mbr-pwrc.usgs.gov/id/framlst/i6130id.html

LESSON 44: RABBITS

www.webbedworks.com/messingerwoods/rabbitprofile.htm
This is a general information site.

www.norfolk.k12.ma.us/students/macchi/cottontail%20rabbit%20
This is a picture of an art project done by two students that might perhaps inspire.

www.enchantedlearning.com/subjects/mammals/farm/Rabbitprintout.shtml
This site has several printouts related to rabbits, even a rabbit quiz. There is also a K-3 unit about rabbits.

LESSON 56: THE HARVEST MOUSE

www.nsrl.ttu.edu/tmot1/reitfulv.htm

www.abdn.ac.uk/mammal/harvest.htm
This site contains pictures of a harvest mouse beside its nest.

www.saskschools.ca/~gregory/animals/mice.html
This site contains more pictures of harvest mice beside their nests.

www.ingramcontent.com/pod-product-compliance
Lightning Source LLC
Chambersburg PA
CBHW080533090426
42733CB00015B/2570